Action Words

Verbs

Anita Ganeri

Heinemann Library
Chicago, Illinois

www.capstonepub.com
Visit our website to find out
more information about
Heinemann-Raintree books.

To order:
☎ Phone 888-454-2279
💻 Visit www.capstonepub.com
to browse our catalog and order online.

Edited by Daniel Nunn, Rebecca Rissman, and Sian Smith
Designed by Joanna Hinton-Malivoire
Picture research by Tracy Cummins
Original illustrations © Capstone Global Library
Illustrated by Joanna Hinton-Malivoire
Production by Eirian Griffiths
Originated by Capstone Global Library Ltd
Printed and bound in China by South China Printing
Company Ltd

15 14 13 12 11
10 9 8 7 6 5 4 3 2 1

Library of Congress Cataloging-in-Publication Data
Ganeri, Anita, 1961-
   Action words : verbs / Anita Ganeri.
      p. cm.—(Getting to grips with grammar)
   Includes bibliographical references and index.
ISBN 978-1-4329-5810-7 (hbk) ISBN 978-1-4329-5817-6 (pbk)
1. English language—Verb—Juvenile literature. 2. English
language—Grammar—Juvenile literature. I. Title.
PE1271.G36 2011
428.1—dc22   2011014971

Acknowledgments
We would like to thank the following for permission to reproduce
photographs and artworks: istockphoto pp.14 (© iofoto), 24 (©
Thomas M Perkins), 27 (© devil); Shutterstock p5 (© Leah-Anne
Thompson), 6 (© Kitch Bain), 8 (© Roca), 9 (© Angelika Smile), 10
(© Guido Vrola), 11 (© Blend Images), 17 (© Julien Tromeur), 18
(© naluwan), 19 (© luchschen), 20 (© Amanda Perkins), 21 (©
Uryadnikov Sergey), 25 (© Galina Barskaya), 26 (© neff), 28, 29
(© Elena Elisseeva), 30a (© AYAKOVLEV.COM), 30b (© Nate A.),
30c (© hektoR).

Every effort has been made to contact copyright holders of any
material reproduced in this book. Any omissions will
be rectified in subsequent printings if notice is given to
the publisher.

Disclaimer
All the Internet addresses (URLs) given in this book were
valid at the time of going to press. However, due to the
dynamic nature of the Internet, some addresses may have
changed, or sites may have changed or ceased to exist
since publication. While the author and Publishers regret any
inconvenience this may cause readers, no responsibility for
any such changes can be accepted by either the author or
the Publishers.

Contents

Some words are shown in bold, **like this**.
You can find them in the glossary on page 31.

What Is Grammar?

Grammar is a set of rules that helps you to write and speak a language. Grammar is important because it helps people to understand each other.

in school I to morning. walk the

Without grammar, this **sentence** doesn't make sense.

In grammar, words are divided up into different types. They are called parts of speech. They show how words are used. This book is about the parts of speech called **verbs**.

Grammar turns the jumbled-up words into a sentence.

I walk to school in the morning.

What Is a Verb?

A **verb** is a doing or action word. It tells us what a person or thing is doing.

Winston bakes a cake.

"Bakes" is a verb. It tells you what Winston is doing.

Birds fly in the sky.

This is a sentence.
It has a verb ("fly").

Birds in the sky.

This is not
a sentence.
It does not
have a verb.

Every **sentence** needs to have a verb
in it. Otherwise, it doesn't make sense.
Look at the two examples above.

Spot the Verb

Look at this list of words. Can you see all the **verbs** in the list? Remember that a verb is a doing word.

jump

climb

castle

eat

smelly

sing

"Jump," "climb," "eat," and "sing" are verbs. "Castle" and "smelly" are *not* verbs.

Look at the two **sentences** below. How many verbs can you spot? There is one verb in the first sentence and there are two in the second sentence.

> **I play the piano.**
>
> **Dogs bark and chase cats.**

In the first sentence, the verb is "play." In the second sentence, the verbs are "bark" and "chase."

Subjects and Objects

In a **sentence**, a **verb** has to have a subject. The subject is the person or thing doing the action. The subject comes before the verb.

The rocket flew **through space.**

"The rocket" is the subject. "Flew" is the verb.

Ben builds a sandcastle.

"Ben" is the subject, "builds" is the verb, "a sandcastle" is the object.

In some sentences, the verb has an object as well. The object is the person or thing the verb is being done to. The object comes after the verb.

I, You, He/She/It

"I," "you," and "he/she/it" are called the first, second, and third person. You often have to change how you use a **verb** depending on whether your **sentence** is using the first, second, or third person.

(First person) I am **happy.**

(Second person) You **are happy.**

(Third person) He/she/it **is happy.**

This shows how the verb "to be" is used in the first, second, and third person.

The first, second, and third person can be **singular** or **plural**. "I," "you," "he," "she," and "it" are all singular. Singular means one person or thing.

I am flying a kite.

"I" is the first person singular.

"She" is the third person singular.

She is reading a book.

We, You, They

"We," "you," and "they" are the **plural** of the first, second, and third person. Plural means more than one person or thing.

(First person) We **are happy.**

(Second person) You **are happy.**

(Third person) They **are happy.**

These sentences are using the first, second, and third person plural.

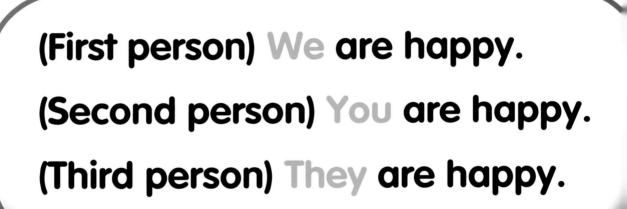

I am picking some flowers.

This is written in the first person. The plural is "We are picking some flowers."

This is written in the third person. The plural is "They are playing soccer."

She is playing soccer.

Look at the two **sentences** above. They are **singular**. Can you rewrite them in the plural? Can you also say which person they are written in?

What Is a Tense?

Verbs also change when they describe things happening at different times. These changes are called **tenses**. The main tenses are the **present**, **past**, and **future**.

I ride a horse.

I rode a horse.

I will ride a horse.

The first sentence is in the present tense.
The second sentence is in the past tense.
The third sentence is in the future tense.

The tense of a verb tells you the time something happened. Look at these three **sentences**. Can you tell the tense?

We watched **television.**

Lucy smiles**.**

I will catch **a fish.**

The first sentence is in the past tense.
The second sentence is in the present tense.
The third sentence is in the future tense.

Present Tense

The **present tense** means that something is happening now. The two **sentences** below use the present tense. Can you think of any other examples?

I sing a song.

I drink some juice.

Both of these sentences are in the present tense.

There is also the present **continuous** tense. This is used to show that the action is going on for a while.

I am singing a song.

I am drinking some juice.

Both of these sentences are in the present continuous tense.

Past Tense

The **past tense** means that something has already happened. The **sentences** below use the past tense. Can you think of any more examples?

The giraffe munched **some leaves.**

The boat sank**.**

Both of these sentences are in the past tense.

The giraffe **was munching** some leaves.

The boat **was sinking**.

Both of these sentences are in the past continuous tense.

There is also the past **continuous** tense. This is used to show that the action went on for a while.

Changing Verbs

To make the **past tense**, you often add "ed" to **verbs**. For example, "clean" becomes "cleaned." But some verbs make the "ed" ending in a different way.

Present tense	Past tense
bat	batted
fit	fitted
cry	cried
bury	buried

With these verbs, you have to add or change some letters before you can add "ed" to make the past tense.

Some verbs completely change in the past tense. They are often verbs that you use a lot.

Present tense	Past tense
buy	bought
grow	grew
keep	kept
hide	hid
swim	swam
run	ran

You just have to learn the past tenses of these verbs. There is no easy rule to help you work out what they should be.

Future Tense

The **future tense** means that something will happen in the future. The **sentences** below use the future tense. Can you think of any more examples?

Both of these sentences are in the future tense.

I will do some shopping.

You will play tennis.

I will be doing **some shopping.**

You will be playing **tennis.**

Both of these sentences are in the future continuous tense.

There is also the future **continuous** tense. This is used to show that the action will go on for a while.

Helping Verbs

The **verb** "to have" is called a helping verb. It is used with other words to help make the different **tenses**.

The words "have" and "will have" come from the verb "to have."

They have worked hard.

He will have missed his train.

The verb "to be" is another helping verb. It is also used with other words to help make the different tenses.

The dog was barking.

A spider is hiding in the tub.

The words "was" and "is" come from the verb "to be."

Active and Passive

You can use a **verb** in two different ways. One way is to use it as an **active** verb. Using an active verb is a strong, direct way of saying something.

Here, the subject "Dad" did the verb "watered." The verb is active.

Dad watered the plants.

The plants were watered by Dad.

Here, the subject "plants" were having the verb done to them. The verb is passive.

The other way of using a verb is to use it as a **passive** verb. Using a passive verb is a gentler, less direct way of saying something.

Find the Verbs

Look carefully at the pictures below. Can you think of a **verb** to go with each one?

Answers
a: dance
b: eat or smile
c: climb

Glossary

active a way of using a verb in a strong, direct way

continuous something that goes on for a while

future something that may or will happen

grammar a set of rules that helps you to speak or write clearly

passive a way of using a verb in a gentler, less direct way

past something that has already happened

plural meaning more than one person or thing

present something that is happening now

sentence a group of words that makes sense on its own

singular meaning one person or one thing

tense different form of a verb that tells you when something happened

verb doing or action word

Find Out More

Books

Cleary, Brian P. *Slide and Slurp, Scratch and Burp: More About Verbs.* Minneapolis, MN: Lerner, 2010.

Dahl, Michael. *If You Were a Verb.* Mankato, MN: Picture Window Books, 2007.

Websites

http://media.arcademicskillbuilders.com/games/viper/viper.swf?0
This entertaining Website helps readers identify the correct tense to use with a fun, exciting game.

www.bradleys-english-school.com/online/jigword/jigpast1.html
This site challenges readers to complete a puzzle filling in the correct past tense words.

Index